"Marianna Pease's series of s_____ _____ _____ _____ through the darkest time of Pease's life – a new baby, a divorce, a pandemic – with grace, humor and a heaping dose of healing. Pease writes from the heart about motherhood, marriage, heartbreak and resolution in a book that will not only help her heal, but will also help other women coping with divorce. It is rare to find a book so beautifully written that is poignant, relatable and full of resources. As a therapist who works with women navigating divorce, I can't wait to recommend this book to my clients."

Oona Metz, LICSW, www.oonametz.com

"Pandemic Mom is a beautiful, expansive journey through pain and it will leave you full of healing energy – it's a balm for the grieving, overwhelmed mama stuck in unknowns, a needed permission slip to express unspoken truths, a map towards light & hope and a practical guide to find those first steps. Marianna lovingly, knowingly, takes your tired mama hand, your lost mama heart and gives courage to reach into those dark places inside where the untangling of your own story begins and the rebuilding can start."

Lily Herman, www.lilianherman.com

"Marianna gets vulnerable in her writings about her personal experiences as a single mother going through divorce. She gets up front and personal about the challenges of reclaiming your life on your own, while at the same time grieving and letting go of the past. I commend her for telling her truth and speaking up for women everywhere going through similar circumstances. As a therapist, I commend her for showing up and showing the vulnerability of her experience with the willingness to give a voice to all those quietly suffering. With her insight and humor, she takes readers into what it was like going through a divorce as a single mom through her eyes and perspective. Her experience, highs and lows, as well as hope for other single moms out there, is a good source of knowledge for those on their own personal journey of self-discovery. She provides wonderful resources to help others along their own path. I recommend this book for all those wanting to travel the journey of divorce and parenting together."

Valentina Verani, www.valentinaveranilmhc.com

"Oh, how I wish my mother had this book during her divorce! Marianna shares from her heart with such care, conviction, and courage about a topic that can be so ugly. Her humor is so refreshing, and she has such a relatable way with words. You feel as if you're both curled together on the couch, sipping tea, and healing together."

Victoria Nielsen, mama, healer & empowerment coach, www.spiritmamas.com

PANDEMIC MOM

**Meditations on New
Motherhood During the
Pandemic & During Divorce**

MARIANNA
SALTONSTALL PEASE

Copyright © 2023 by Marianna Saltonstall Pease

All rights reserved. No part of this publication may be reproduced, distributed or transmitted in any form or by any means without permission of the publisher, except in the case of brief quotations referencing the body of work and in accordance with copyright law.

The information given in this book should not be treated as a substitute for professional medical advice; always consult a medical practitioner. Any use of information in this book is at the reader's discretion and risk. Neither the author nor the publisher can be held responsible for any loss, claim or damage arising out of the use, or misuse, of the suggestions made, the failure to take medical advice or for any material on third party websites.

Cover image photo credit: Kim Conant

Edited By: Roland Pease & Jesse Smart

Book Design: Leah Kent

ISBN 978-1-916529-09-0 Paperback

ISBN 978-1-916529-10-6 Ebook

The Unbound Press
www.theunboundpress.com

Hey unbound one!

Welcome to this magical book brought to you by The Unbound Press.

At The Unbound Press we believe that when women write freely from the fullest expression of who they are, it can't help but activate a feeling of deep connection and transformation in others. When we come together, we become more and we're changing the world, one book at a time!

This book has been carefully crafted by both the contributors and publisher with the intention of inspiring you to move ever more deeply into who you truly are.

We hope that this book helps you to connect with your Unbound Self and that you feel called to pass it on to others who want to live a more fully expressed life.

With much love,
Nicola Humber

Founder of The Unbound Press
www.theunboundpress.com

For my Daughter. I love you all day.

CONTENTS

Foreword - xi
Part One - My Story - 1
Part Two - Strength, Hope & Healing - 47

Journaling Prompts - 105
Organizations and Resources - 121

Acknowledgments - 125
About the Author - 127

"What didn't you do to bury me,

but you forgot that I was a seed..."

– Dinos Christianopoulos

Foreword

Dear Reader,

Thank you for being here. I'm going to jump right in.

This book is a courageous act for me. It includes both the writing I used to heal myself, by taking my power back, and everything compiled that I have learned as a new mother during the pandemic, during divorce. My deepest heartfelt wish is that in sharing, I can pay it forward, and perhaps offer some sliver of hope to someone still deep within the darkness of their own journey. So this is my offering back to the world from the trenches of the dark night of the soul that was my divorce.

So, what happened to me?

In 2019, I conceived my first child (a lifelong dream of mine to become a mother) with my then-husband of a year, whom I had known throughout my twenties. We were married in 2018. There was a double rainbow at our wedding. Within six months, the pandemic hit. We had an emergency leak in our place in Boston that needed repairs and a full construction demo, leaving our home inhabitable. My mother swooped me under her wing, and I decided to stay with my parents in Vermont during my third trimester to stay safe with my unborn baby. I switched my OB care to midwives in Vermont. These were the early days of Covid, when people were frequently dying and the facts of the disease were still new.

In June 2020, I gave birth to a 9.4-pound healthy baby girl with midwives in an unmedicated birth.

When my child was two weeks old, my husband and I left Vermont to stay in Brighton, MA, in an Airbnb, while our condo's renovation was delayed by the early days of Covid. It was then that the underlying troubles peaked in the marriage. There is more to say. Layers. But some things will remain private out of respect for my family. This is not a tell all. The story that I will share is about my own healing.

In August 2020, I separated from my husband when my daughter was two months old, with the intention to work things out, which went steeply downhill, turned into legal bills, filing for divorce, and a lot of trauma. Mind you, this was after fighting to save the marriage, leaving no stone unturned for years in couples counseling. I left because I had no choice. I needed to protect my daughter from our conflict and focus on her care. It was initiated from a point of survival.

I took care of my infant alone in quarantine in those early days when I was scared for my unvaccinated family to come in due to no vaccines and high risks with the virus. Eventually, I was able to hire some childcare help. Shout out to Yona and Shelli.

Three years later, my divorce was finalized after nearly going to trial.

After three years of silence, I speak.

And I speak not from spite, not for gossip or revenge. I speak from the heart. Divorce can be traumatic and a serious reckoning. New motherhood is a rebirth for the mother, and all of this can lead to true healing and self-discovery if you go deep and do the work, which of course is not fancy stuff, but it's the pressure that makes diamonds, right? The grit? Not fun. Only when you have had to be strong when you don't want to be will you resonate with this. When others say, "I don't know how you did it," the answer is, well, I had no choice. And it's not the path I would have chosen. But here we are. I have a daughter. And I will do anything for my daughter.

My intention is to share the depths of my pain and highlights of humor to comfort or give perspective to anyone who needs it.

If you are a new mother, or are contemplating separation or divorce, please know I am you, I see you, you are not alone and the darkness can be overcome with grace, and with time. You can take it from me, because I just assumed after three years, my divorce would maybe be the first never to end. My attitude was "I'll believe it when I see it." And still, one day, I got a call from my lawyer, "Well, it's over." I was in shock. The excitement slowly rolled in like fog, as did the freedom, as I took back my power little by little.

There will come a day, even if you cannot fathom it, when you wake up freed, lighter, ready to move on, and sick of talking about your divorce. Your energy will change, the suffocation will lift. You will unfreeze and emerge from the dark times. These are not empty words. I have seen it, time and time again, as members "graduate" from my divorce support group.

And my turn came too. The turn came for me. Sometimes it feels like I time-warped to this point. How is my pandemic baby now about to turn three? I want to cry when I think of myself at the start of this process. That's how dark it was. I was speechless in my pain at the start. I had no words. None of it made any sense. It all had to be untangled. My pain, my words, my past, my legal plans, my grief, my new identity...

It is terrifying to speak up, but someone might need these words. I would have at the beginning.

At my lowest low, I thought my husband would return for me. He did not. At my rock bottom, I thought my life had somehow been switched out for a new one. It made no sense. I could not fathom how all of this could have happened. I never would have let it get this bad or even dreamed it could have. Language helped me the most in constructing my narrative, in addition to support groups, therapy, medication as needed (I'm being honest here – someone needs to hear it and have this normalized), and keeping the hope.

And guess what? I'm not done healing. I'm intentionally writing this from the heal-ING place in the journey – isn't that more relatable anyways?

And now:

A word about my child's father: He is a good father, and though we were not the right compatible fit, we both suffered enormously. Though we did not work out, the loss is nonetheless tragic. Even despite the suffering, this was a man I loved, my child's father. I will say nothing negative of him here, out of respect for him and my daughter.

May you have the courage to awaken to your personal power in time.

With love,

Marianna

PART ONE

♥

MY STORY

Church Bells

Maybe if we had married in a church

Instead of a barn.

Maybe if we had traveled the world first.

Yet we did some.

I'll trade you back my twenties, if I can keep the baby.

Maybe the double rainbow was a warning,

"Only two, of you three, will be family at one time."

I can hear the church bells from our honeymoon.

I'll buy one fat new memory to soak up the first layer.

Oh look, they sell scarves here! Oh look, they sell jewels. You don't need these, he says.

And now I want to return the happy memories. I don't know where to store them in the shelving unit.

Reclaim it, the girls say.

The tokens don't bother me like the days we shared in their entirety.

The span of days longer than bodies of water, whole rivers that cross countries, the lengths of memories we shared, just to find out, No. No.

No more conflict. Not in front of my daughter.

I sold my wedding shoes on The RealReal. I got $7.50. You wore your wedding shoes to family court, the ones I bought you, and you didn't look me in the eye – so I looked down and, well, I recognized the double brown buckles.

I'll trade you that one fish dinner in Positano, I'll trade you New Years in Havana, I'll trade you my 30th birthday, I'll trade you any dim sum brunch you wanna eat, okay? Any Marvel movie three hours long, okay? Get off my back. I'll trade you church bells for the grief I have swallowed with my entire life. I'll trade you dancing shoes for the grief I have swallowed with my entire life. I'll trade you one fish dinner – the one where you looked blissed up in the photo – that one my friend found in the basement and told me I looked beautiful, but no, I have to regenerate, oh my sweet husband who perished like a snowman in the rain, photo in the basement. I'll trade you that wedding, that marriage, for the sound of peace ringing from a pew, from a choir, from a courtyard, from the rooftops, or from YouTube. Bells from YouTube. Bells from YouTube, sound effect of bells from YouTube like an alarm to call out enough is enough.

Pandemic Mom

I always thought it would be extraordinarily fun to push my baby in a baby carriage. The first time I did this I was wearing blue plastic hospital gloves. The CDC hadn't announced yet in June of 2020 that Covid-19 did not live on surfaces. Hi, I am Pandemic Mom.

When I was nine months pregnant, the nurse called at nine p.m. on a Sunday to inform me I may have to give birth alone. "I am prepared to do that," I said. Hi, I am Pandemic Mom.

One of the questions I wrote down while pregnant to ask my midwife was: Will I have to give birth wearing a face mask? Hi, I am Pandemic Mom.

My first video of my newborn has two nurses attending to her wearing face shields as she cried out in a little newborn squeak. Hi, I am Pandemic Mom.

We canceled the baby shower after we planned it. No one owned a face mask yet. My best friends did a Zoom instead where they read me some poems, God bless them. Hi, I am Pandemic Mom.

My infant used to play peekaboo with the face masks and snap them. I have Clorox wipes in my diaper bag. Hi, I am Pandemic Mom.

I Was Never Your Wife

I took your hand in front of a room full of witnesses

But, I was never your wife.

I bore your child, but no,

I took your name, but no,

I was devoted, but no.

There was no husband, and so,

I was never your wife.

You said today, on the four-way call with our lawyers,

that you could blah blah blah, if your wife had let you blah blah blah,

And I wondered who she was, the nice wife of a husband.

Certainly not me.

You see I?

I was planning on it, but in the end,

as it turned out,

there was no marriage, and so,

I was

never your wife.

The Thick of Winter

For a long time, I thought he was coming back. Then for a while, I thought it was possible for him to come back. Then I prayed and joined a church in the thick of winter. Then, panic. How could I have lost my husband?

For a while, I thought maybe my reality had been switched out for a new one. When I missed him, I hugged our newborn baby. He would not return my calls.

The pandemic didn't help. The world was changed. Family could not just come visit me. I couldn't just pop out to get my nails done. I had to face my pain.

A year in, I had a check-in with the group leader of my divorce support group. I said to her I wasn't sure how to measure if I was making any progress.

"You have made progress," she said, "when you first started, you thought your husband was coming back."

I see now he will never return for me. More things than death can end a journey.

My mother always said there is no limit to how strong you have to be.

The Fourth Trimester

When I was nine months pregnant, I read how to nurture oneself during the postpartum period. I took notes in the margins of the book on ways to bond with your new family, rally your village, I read about nourishing soups to cook from around the world traditions. Ha ha. Never once did I think of bone broth!

During the period of time where one normally sets up the nursery, I took long walks down my parents' driveway in quarantine. In the videos, I get more and more pregnant while discussing which grandmother I wanted to name the baby after.

I did a lot of things while I waited for my husband to make it to the birth. I colored in a coloring book. I studied birthing meditations. I taught myself to french braid. He did make it to the birth. I wish I could have named her after family. And what does it matter if you can french braid, really.

We didn't have a gender reveal. We had to cancel my baby shower even though we had already sent out invitations. No one owned a mask yet. There's more to say here, but honestly, what is one more missed opportunity?

We did not try for a second child. By her first birthday, I had legal bills and well-meaning friends telling me it was a "bold move to separate with a two-month-old." Me keeping it brief but telling the truth: "I had no choice."

It all does bother me.

I did, while pregnant, make a list of all my postpartum essentials, so bottom line, I guess you could underline this:

A swaddle with a zipper is great for the hospital

Screw the birthing music

Screw the heavy diaper bag

Screw the infant shoes that will never fit

Factor in a good herbal sitz spray, a meal delivery service, and plan to be surrounded by women who love you.

Apple Squeeze

Every night at five p.m., I push my infant daughter to the playground in the stroller. Every night after going to the playground, we walk home to our empty house. We are one family of two. I've got her, but no one's got me. Yeah, yeah, I've got me. But still the house is empty.

Don't ask me what I do for fun. Right now, all you can see is that my face looks pinched in photos. Maybe I should let my hair down. Don't tell me I look beautiful, beauty is an energy. It will regenerate.

Walking home from the park and my daughter is having an apple fruit squeeze. The nice thing about having an apple fruit squeeze when you are one year old is that when you are done, you just drop it. I always dreamed of being a mother.

And then I see a couple silhouetted by the setting sun walking just ahead of us and my brain turns to mush. I too dressed up for dinner once.

I don't know what people mean when they say it's okay to not be okay. They must be talking about a bad day. I tried crying it out but the tears never stopped. I vowed to never do that again.

I get the concept that one should seek out a stable, emotionally present partner, but how am I supposed to feel seen in that shit? I am suffering. Hey, can you mirror that back to me?

They say the thing you are most avoiding is the step you most need to take to free up your life. For me – it's inner child work. I would rather eat a million bees.

And yet, here I am, learning to be alone and fine with it, not by choice. I guess the lesson is courage. I guess the script is bravery.

My neighborhood association sends out an email that pops to the top of my inbox:

They're fixing the GASLIGHTS.

My intention is to wish a voice to the voiceless.

The Leather Anniversary

Today is our third wedding anniversary. Three. We celebrated our first by getting dim sum, going to the MFA, and sitting at a bar eating rock shrimp. Last year you came home at four a.m. with a grocery store rose while I sat on the couch nursing our two-month-old. And this year you are gone. There is nothing to celebrate on the third anniversary of a marriage during divorce.

At our wedding during dinner, everyone ran out of the barn to watch the entire span of a double rainbow. I remember thinking the morning after, when I woke up and got breakfast alone, that no one could ever take this day away from us. He didn't mean for this. I did not mean for this. It's like we should have seen a psychic instead of a marriage counselor. But then again, he used to say he saw a storm coming and I dreamt our house caught fire.

Last night I searched the eyes of everyone in our wedding photos, looking for clues. I lost him as if he slipped under the ocean. I lost him as if we got separated traveling abroad. I lost him. If only there was something I did not try left to do.

Traditionally on the third anniversary, people exchange gifts of leather. We used to talk about someday getting a leather couch. When I met you, you wore a leather cuff. Please return for your daughter if not for me. The most romantic thing in the world must be to have a family.

Voicemail (My Birth Story)

When I was pregnant, I was interested in how nobody could explain to me exactly what giving birth actually felt like. I am talking about the pain. Which is a hard thing to pinpoint in words anyway, but what I was really trying to determine was: How familiar would the experience ultimately be?

My first contraction was at lunch. I had spent the winter and spring at my family's house in the woods as the pandemic broke, walking up and down their long driveway, listening to the voices of unseen bullfrogs who appeared out of nowhere. When the frogs suddenly disappeared altogether, the weather was very hot, it was my due date, and baby girl was ready to come through.

My plan was to labor at home. At first, it just felt like mild period cramps. This was exactly the kind of data I was waiting for. When the pain got worse, I hopped in the bathtub and he fed me strawberries off a large clay platter while I laughed in embarrassment at how well things were going. I ate maybe three at his suggestion.

There is a weird bit about labor where the woman reaches a certain threshold, declares herself ready for the hospital, a point that she alone is able to explain that she has reached, and no one quite believes her. Is she really ready? She said she was ready. Could it be too soon? Or worse – too late? Can we trust a woman in the throes of such a turbulent state?

I rode the thirty minutes to the hospital propped up on my hands in the back seat of my car. For a portion of the drive, we bumped along a dirt road where there was no way I could brace my own self from my own insides. The intake nurse accepted me by the skin of my teeth, and I told them, good, I would have waited in the driveway.

As it turns out, no one can tell you how much birth hurts. For me, a birth without pain medication of a nearly nine-and-a-half pound baby was extremely painful, though tolerable and oddly not altogether foreign. Sure, I had a second-degree tear, but the worst part was the unfamiliar sensation of internal churning as my child got into position, for which I now get why doulas talk about "counter-pressure."

Actually, the worst bits came later, when I took care of my newborn alone. These were the uncharted territories of which I did not yet know my own threshold. You could call it a lot of things: bullshit, a reckoning, a dark night of the soul, time will tell.

My child is a gift.

I screamed that child out of me like a witch in the night. Whatever I had left unspoken was voiced then.

You can prepare for birth to the same degree in which you can prepare for any unknown if you are able to see it coming. You can read books, you can talk to friends, you can hire some kind of trusted chaperone. But then sometimes too, in the thick of it, all one's calls go straight to voicemail and you just have to trust your own breath and heartbeat to get to the other side.

Sometimes you are the portal and sometimes you are going through a portal. Sometimes the portal has to nurture the portal. I became a mother. We live alone now. I take care of her and I take care of me.

A Nun Walks By

I always said to myself, "Well, at least if my life turns out to complete shit, I could always become a nun." I had meant it as a joke. But here I am. Alone, standing at the changing table with my infant daughter, in a pandemic, separated and remote from all family, friends, and my one-time husband. And a nun walks by outside the window. She is heading down the avenue on a pretty day out for a walk.

I'm up at four a.m. nursing and I Google, "Why is my four-month-old buzzing?" I read it is "actually a developmental milestone and a sign of language development"– certainly an optimistic view for the concern that I had actually plugged into Google: my child is spitting.

I am spinning on my exercise bike because I haven't yet figured out how to be an outdoor runner. My doctor says it's true, belly buttons are "never quite the same after childbirth," and I say okay, I'll just wear a one-piece swimsuit like all the other moms – and she says, "or just Body Beautiful." She says it like it is one word and I realize she's right – to just enjoy the beach no matter what the hell has happened. I remember this while trying to fit into an old sweater. Sigh. I glance up. A nun walks by outside my window. The same nun. The same walk, a different day.

We also walk. Up and down the same side street because it is a global pandemic and Newbury Street is spilling over with outdoor dining and the esplanade is ripe with a sudden explosion of outdoor runners (should I try it?). When my baby is nearly six months old, we walk to the drop-off box by the Boston Public Library and cast our vote. A few days later, someone tried to set that box on fire but I check online and my vote appears to have been processed.

Really though, does everything always have to be such a close call? I have already decided that if my child ends up being "a spitter" in her preschool, I will tell the teacher to "ask her father." I really admire her emerging personality.

I alternate between biking and also, at times, eating almond butter with a spoon. I wish I had a vice, I really do. Today I am biking and I see the nun again. I'm not even really sure if there's a convent nearby but it's been three times now that I've seen her.

When I got married, some other married women told me that one of the advantages to having a spouse is having someone to keep you accountable. If you live alone, you can easily take up strange habits. I've recently started to wonder which of my habits could be the strange one. Maybe it is that I am always wondering what the meaning of things are that should actually be taken at face value.

Today I read in a targeted internet article that you can't just go become a nun if you have been married. So shit. This is too bad for me, but I do appreciate the absolute certainty.

I will seek hope in another venture.

Hi, I'm in the Wrong Support Group!

Sort of handsome, biblically, "allowed to divorce" man lists his interests on Meetup as: hiking and "beautiful women." Huh. I revisit what I put for mine, and it says: yoga and breastfeeding.

You wouldn't believe some of the damaging shit I accidentally logged on from Meetup just thinking I was just "doing a little self-care." Hell, I'd get more emotional support from taking a Peloton class!

One night, I got off a phone call with my mom to log into a Zoom divorce group where they had us all turn off our cameras to watch a DMV-style video about who, in Christianity, is allowed to divorce, and apparently, you can't remarry if (something something something) and this poor fifty-year-old man seemed pretty crushed by it. And you know what? I didn't even worry about typing "bye guys" (in the chat). I just logged right off to go breastfeed!

And did you know that this time last year, I was taking calls to interview attorneys while bouncing a newborn? I didn't hire the first one because he referred to signing the fee agreement as "consummating our relationship." And I don't know about you, but what the fuck, man? I guess this is just how my January is going to keep going!

Tell my new Zoom mom friends how I'm doing and realize this isn't supposed to be so much about me. (Just trying to stay positive!) I do wish though that they had the decency to stop complaining about their husbands.

Or worse, referring to them as "their rock." Makes me forget not to want a husband too. I dream of a day where I could be a little less strong all the time.

Hi, I'm in the wrong support group!

Who is June Cleaver?

What do you wear to an in-person custody court hearing? Well, my lawyer said you just dress like a mom. Look like a mom.

I consider this. I am a mom. I look like a mom. I don't have to try to look like a mom. I don't have enough time to chop up a salad and I've been up feeding a baby for a year at four a.m. Why would my jeans fit? Do you think I can still work a crop top?

I keep asking around. Do you have any knee-length black skirts? No. I've never been to court. Why would I have a black knee-length skirt? Oh look! I have one but it doesn't fit anymore.

Dress like June Cleaver, my lawyer says. Who? I say.

Oh June Cleaver!! My mom says!

I Google June Cleaver. Her picture pulls up a 1950s housewife with short curly hair (mine is straight) who wears clothing from the fifties with an apron.

How do I take inspiration from this?

Wear pearls, my mom says.

Babymoon Gunman

It was the last night of our Miami babymoon. January 2020. I had a sundress on and my baby bump, for the first time, out. I was ready for dinner.

"Let's try Wynwood!" I said. I'd never been. It looked trendy. I read it was up and coming, which I guess just means in the process of gentrification.

"Sure, why not?" he said without looking up from a video game he was playing at the hotel room desk.

We pulled up with our hardtop Mercedes convertible. Thanks, Sixt rentals! The area looked a little off.

We parked the car. We didn't see the restaurant. He started to walk. We walked a few blocks and saw a car parked down an alley. We walked around the block and saw not some but zero signs of the restaurant.

And then, we saw something else. The block filled with cop cars.

"They're looking for the gunman," my husband told me as he ran to join the cops leaving me standing on the sidewalk in full pregnant display. "I'd like to go home," I said.

After some time, we drove to a tourist area, parked the rental car in a garage and walked to get dinner in a food court.

"Fuck Wynwood," I said. And then to try and appear positive... "Should we name her Winifred?" I said as a joke. I was fawning, in retrospect.

That night I woke up crying in my sleep.

I later donated the sundress, briefly opening my mouth to explain to someone why, then closing it.

'Till Cross-Examination Do Us Part

The good news is that someday this will end.

The bad news is that yesterday at my pre-trial hearing at Suffolk family court, the judge asked our availability for trial dates.

The good news is I have an amazing, happy and healthy two-and-a-half-year-old daughter.

The bad news is I was recently cross-examined in two four-hour-long depositions about my prenup while he watched on a Zoom screen with his camera off, and, after two and a half years of divorcing her father, I am now waiting for trial dates.

'Till cross-examination do us part, I guess.

The good news is the glass is half full. I've found a combination of vitamins, exercises, naps, work and social flow that seems to all really vibe. I apply self-tanner. I go for runs. My haircut is cute. And I appear to have lost the baby weight.

The bad news is after two years of litigation in a high-conflict custody case, in a short-term marriage where he signed a prenup – I'm waiting for my trial dates.

In the words of nobody:

Good going.

My Only Talent Is Dress Up

Back when I sold vintage clothing as my job, I used to joke that my only talent was dress up. Partly serious. But now? I am known only for my daughter.

Baby girl and I make a splash. There are few others at the pool, no passing dog walker who does not stop to hang. She wears her sunglasses and strawberry bucket hat to shade her baby cheeks. How is her garden? What did she eat today? A donut peach!! When I wave to the same folks, later even in the same day, in the evening, when my daughter is at her father's, they squint. Who is that lady – do we know her? Could that be the single mother?

"Some people use their child as an accessory," a girl tells me after seeing her great outfit. Without thinking, I answer: Oh, I am hers.

My tombstone will read without question: She was only good at dress up. She had one daughter.

A Tired Woman

Thursday, I was pretty tired.

Friday, I was pretty tired.

Saturday, I was pretty tired.

Sunday, I was smoked. A mombie. A bruise from walking into a baby gate here, some diaper cream under my nails there.

Sure, I'll never sleep again. Sure, I'll be a mother without her father.

Monday, I was hot lava. Not today! I want to eat and nap.

Tuesday was a rinse repeat.

Wednesday was a serve and enjoy. Why are the pandemic moms meeting to scream in a park, you say? Because caretaking in isolation is a marathon task in a closed container. Of course the nuclear family is a joke. Why would the village exist within one woman?

And what joy are you going to find alone? What joy can my daughter and I drum up today alone? Certainly some. I put on my bathrobe. "Nice coat, Mama!" She walks to the window and tells me she sees a fox. It is a long-haired city dog. I tell her I know what she means.

Blank's Dad

Well, you can call him your ex-husband. Your ex. Your "exiting husband," your "ex-hole," the ladies in divorce group suggest.

None of this feels right. This is a man I loved. My child's father.

I contemplate calling him by his first name but it feels a little jarring to say it out loud, like a violation of my personal verbal peace.

EX-HUSBAND has a severity to it that exceeds my current ability to process my own situation. I was just getting used to telling people my new last name. Will I really, once this divorce is all squared away and sorted, have an ex-husband? I suppose so. Someone mentions she knows someone who calls the dad the sperm donor. We laugh but this is terrible.

You call him "_____'s dad." Finally a woman calmly lets me know in church group.

Thank you, I say. Now he has a name. This feels decent. Blank's dad it is.

Mom Bod

Why, though, is my post-baby bellybutton the size of a walnut?

"A Walmart?" My friend asks on the phone.

"No, a walnut," I say. But maybe a Walmart is better.

After my husband moved out, I took over his closet with all of my pre-baby clothes and they sat there for a year and a half unworn. At what point do I just declare myself a bigger bitch? But what if, also, thirty pounds heavier is the weight that my body wants to be? Or is that a "limiting belief?" Do I have diastasis recti? Hard to say. I would totally chop a salad if I had the time. Gain 20-30 pounds when pregnant, they said. Whatever. I could not stop gaining 50. Yeah, I get the appeal of the high-waisted thing.

My body did not bounce back.

Diaper Calling

The baby has been repeatedly picking up her diaper rash cream and putting it to her ear.

"Who's calling?" I ask her.

"Mima!" she replies.

In the bathtub, she picks up a red rubber fish and puts it to her ear.

"Who is it?" I ask.

"Mima!" she says with great glee.

I contact my mother. "Mum, the baby is trying to reach you."

She FaceTimes us, "And it works!"

Hers and Hers Rocking Chairs

The day I filed for divorce, I told my best friend on an evening walk while pushing my baby in her stroller that "I feel like a snow globe of emotion I'm just trying not to shake."

Sometimes you have to take the first step forward only because there is no remaining step back. Sometimes the next steps don't appear until you close the door.

I have my grandfather's rocking chair and next to it is my daughter's, a small pink one. We rock and watch the snow fall. We spend the afternoon, my baby and I, in our matching rocking chairs, watching the plump snowflakes fall.

Hers and hers.

One family of two. Everything's the same but the duo.

Holy Grail Baby Items

Zipper swaddle, so you can sleep

Bouncer, so you can shower

Swing, so you can eat

Carrier, so you can answer the door

Stroller, so you can walk

Sitz spray, so you can heal

Some help, so you can sleep

Some help, so you can shower

Sometimes some help, so you can eat

Help, so you can answer the door

Help, so you can walk

Help, so you can heal

Meet the Doula Day

I had it in my head to try for a natural birth. My friend did it. My mom did it. Hell. But mostly my periods have been so excruciatingly painful my whole life, read: "disruptful," I was deeply curious if birth was basically just the same thing.

Spoiler: somewhat, yeah.

Initially, I was signed up to give birth at a downtown hospital, one of the big names, because my longtime OB-GYN worked there. But my so-called "birthing plan," I learned, was not "aligned" with my care provider and hospital.

I learned this at "Meet the Doula Day." An event held by my local yoga studio.

I knew this event was going to go well the second I stepped inside. The receptionist at the check-in counter couldn't find my pregnant ass on the list until they realized I had somehow registered as a doula.

Most people find their doulas on doulamatch.com. I, on the other hand, paid to sign up for a free event and registered as the birthing coach. Cool. Glad they reimbursed me.

I showed up with my best friend. On the floor of the studio sat a circle of doulas and some cushions we would all speed date around. Have YOU ever made a short list on your phone of what you might ask to speed date a doula?

"Oh, that hospital has a lot of c-sections," one doula told me. "They violate a lot of patient requests." "Have you heard about the cascade of interventions?" another doula I interviewed said. "The cascade of what??" I said. Was this getting political?

"What kind of a birth do YOU want?" A doula asked me. The reverse interview.

"Well," I said absentmindedly, thinking of my answer, (How should I know?)

"I was thinking about trying Hypnobabies. It just seems like a cool idea to do HypnoBirthing."

"Those are two different things," the doula said. "Look it up."

"Really?" I said, "Can you explain to me the difference?"

She couldn't. No one can. They are indeed vaguely different. Let me try: One is a system from the nineteen seventies and one is a trademarked program from seemingly Los Angeles. Very similar in every other way.

Ask if she has kids, my friend whispered. MAYBE NOT THAT DOULA, my friend subtly texted. It was clear which doulas were in it to win it, which were moms who needed a side gig (Hi, future me!) and who were a little new but with the full branding package.

The first woman I talked to was by far my perfect doula. And you know what, I hired her and then tragically never got to use her because my whole having-a-baby experience traveled three hours north with the pandemic.

You Can't Win If You Don't Play, Marianna

I disagree.

The First Time / The Last Time

The first time I met my husband, he was wearing a red t-shirt and we walked all over Somerville and took the redline into town to watch the 4th of July festivities on the esplanade. We turned out to be a red flag and I ended up living alone in Boston.

The last time I saw my husband was earlier today when he dropped off my child at four p.m. per the mandated court order and he did not make eye contact.

The first time he told me he loved me, he had just bought me a carton of strawberries at the Farmer's Market and we were sitting at the rooftop pool at his work and he was about to leave for Romania for most of the summer and I was sort of on the edge of tears and he said, "You know I love you, don't you?" And later, a classmate said, "Isn't that sort of like a dog peeing on something as its territory?" But in the moment, I defended him.

The last time we said I love you was when we hugged in the kitchen, which I guess is also the last time we will ever hug. It was when I said to him, "If we can figure this out, we can figure out anything." But then in the end, we figured out it was not a possibility.

It is impossibly sad that nothing lasts forever, or sometimes even for very long.

I Walked Allston/Brighton

The summer that my infant child and I lived in Allston/Brighton in an Airbnb, which also happens to be the summer she was born (wouldn't it be FUN to bring a child home from the hospital to their nursery?), I walked.

My daughter and I walked Allston.

And we walked Brighton.

First, in a baby carrier during or in between naps. Then, in the stroller before the heat of the day. We went to playgrounds just to watch the other babies and be among moms. My child was at the park when she was under one month old. Was I an idiot?

"I can't believe you are here," the moms said to me, "with a baby so young."

I felt it was the only place we really belonged, so I took us there.

My mom came to visit us during a ninety-degree day in July.

"Anna, there are no trees here," she said.

We walked daily to the trees. I shrugged. I was making do. It wasn't my best choice or what I would have chosen.

I remember taking an evening walk (after the heat of the day) on our second wedding anniversary alone with the babe in the front pouch. My mother wishing me a happy anniversary and me sort of registering I had no clue where he was or what he was doing.

Later I recall sitting on the toilet sobbing into my hands as my baby slept. I couldn't quite put my finger on it, but I knew trouble when it stared me down in the final hour, and I was in trouble. I had to put my baby first.

Who The Fuck Is That? Mommy?

And there he was as I turned the corner of the Whole Foods vitamin aisle, at toddler naptime, my estranged husband, leaning over smelling a decorative soap, while my two-year-old daughter ran loose through the produce, kicking an unpurchased pink soccer ball and dropping a bunch of bananas.

Hi guys! I said as I would have to anyone I know if I bumped into them, let alone my own family. He turned to look at me and then he turned his back.

He herded my daughter away from me and out of the store before she could say hi. I stood frozen with my grocery basket filled with one tub of sliced watermelon for my daughter later when she came home from her court-mandated visit. I had come into the Whole Foods because the urologist specialist I had seen that morning had told me to try pumpkin seed oil and aloe vera capsules for my interstitial cystitis, which had flared up from the stress of the divorce after giving birth. As stress-related symptoms often do, they went away after my divorce was finalized.

Forget about co-parenting, who the fuck is that? Mommy?

Messy

The house is messy. The divorce is messy. The toddler is messy. The emotions are messy. The closets are messy. The past is messy. The rebuilding is messy. The mess is messy. Cleaning the mess is also messy. The dishes are messy. The diapers are messy. My hair is messy. The weather is messy. The emails are messy. The calendar is messy. My weight loss journey is messy. My identity is messy. The playpen is messy. The storage unit is messy. My summer plans are messy. The court order is messy. The communication with my child's father is messy. The move upstairs is messy. The cabinets are messy. The schedule gets messy. My sleeping is messy. My handbag is messy. My me time is messy. My long terms plans? A real mess. My patience is messy. The dishes are messy. The laundry is messy. The divorce is messy. A real mess. A real mess.

Momfit of the Day

Today for my Momfit, I will be wearing a matching set with a little bit of yogurt stain on the left shoulder from where my baby lays her head when I try to get her to take her afternoon nap. This outfit fits pretty well, it's olive green so if I'm being self-critical, I can sometimes look in the mirror and feel like a human pickle, but usually I just like to be encased in this structured latex and "ready to go."

Today for my Momfit, I will be wearing a bohemian tunic top with balloon sleeves and some dangle strings knotted with a bead that my toddler baby will approach with the wide eyes of a kitten and say, "oooh!" while trying to bat it. Probably pull one string straight loose. I will wear this to the park with white sneakers feeling fine, like I am perfectly hiding my mom bod, even though I do have a slight awareness that big clothes can go "either way." But for today, I am a bohemian urban priestess. It's fine, I'm a single mother.

Today for my Momfit, I will be wearing a dark mixture of various trash garments that are both ill-fit and feel soft. My fleece, which I usually slap on over pajamas, will be briefly made part of an internal monologue if I can don it to go to the park before I remember that, no, it is "bed clothes." My hair is wet, pulled back in a low twisted bun and for some reason, my concealer is flaking. (The hell?) My eyeliner is good, though, because I have a trusty brand of eyeliner which every bad bitch develops and hell, I'm 34, so pray for me if I didn't at least have this one thing figured out. Oh, anxiety creeps up. Oh, the pandemic is isolating.

Today for my Momfit, I am considering if I should get some type of visor, cap, or sunshade for when we walk to the playground every day because I just literally started applying retinol and hydroelectric oil. I do wear sunscreen in my tinted moisturizer, but truth is I slap on whatever creams I please. I don the hat. More than one adult woman in the street smiles at me. Clearly for the baby but it makes me feel like I am their peer, watching my wrinkles. I want to make some divorced friends. Watch me with this hat!

Today for my Momfit, I am wearing a large tee and leggings with the pockets. My bra is a nursing bra I still own. I weaned her a year ago. I'm not worried about it.

Today for my Momfit, I reach for something familiar. Out of my drawer I slide my olive green latex. Grab the hat, you know I applied a little retinol.

New Witch – Who's This?

I was upset so I pulled a tarot card. It seemed true. But I wasn't ready. It confused me.

I was happy so I pulled an oracle card. It seemed false. But I was ready. I acted impulsively.

I was confused so I called a friend. She had an idea. I listened because I trust her. I wasn't ready. I had to backtrack. Or maybe I just needed to pull a tarot card. Or an angel card to reflect my own true gut which I would later overthink.

I was tired so I went to therapy group. I talked about how tired I was. I needed a nap. It wasted my time and it wasted my money.

Maybe, I thought, if only I could trust my own gut, I could count on my own self to run things by instead of all this heady confusion. The right decision could be argued either way. The wrong feeling can probably be intellectualized to be good enough.

I came to the conclusion, "There is no help." I told my mom. She seemed alarmed. Rightfully so. I had meant helpful advice.

I put my tarot cards away. I put my angel cards away. I pulled out my books. Don't read self-help before bed, my mom said. Read fiction. I don't know who I am. But I used to. Though I dare say I may be, at the core, the same.

Ceiling TV

My favorite part of the toddler dentist is the TV that they have on the ceiling. My second favorite part is when the dentist walks in and says to the pediatric dental hygienist,

"Did she let you do anything?"

I should have known better than to go to the pediatric dentist on the morning of a full moon, but we schedule these things six months out. So off we went.

The dental hygienist was in a really bad mood. Her headband matched her mask, which matched her eyes, teal aqua. She went from standard forced friendly to smiling aggressively when I expressed curiosity on how to get the baby to go to sleep after flossing.

I did not mean to "appear defiant." Whatever, I'll do it, I said.

She turned on the ceiling TV, pointing the remote at the ceiling. She sang along like she hated her life while doing the exam. We completed the task.

The dentist walked in.

"Did she let you do anything?" he said.

Yes, the hygienist said. My daughter had done a great job, she had watched a little ceiling TV. And she got a balloon for this. But it was windy and it bopped her in the head so she kind of disliked it.

As we drove home, I noticed the car in front of us also had a balloon and a toddler, hand waving in the air, in it. I learned my daughter now has eight teeth. Two more to go for a full set of teeth!

Team-Building Family of Two

My family just had a small team-building exercise.

In the house, I caught a huge fly under a plastic seaweed cup.

Then, since I was glued to the wall, so to speak, I asked my two-year-old daughter to go find a piece of paper.

She ran around the house saying, "Piece of paper," and came back with her magic wand.

I found a piece of paper and took the fly to the door.

I asked her to open the door. She tried. I set down the fly, I opened the door, and freed it.

We did double high-fives!

I walked to the kitchen.

Another fly is in the house.

The Idiot's Guide to Coronavirus

"Yeah? Do you have any tips?" My friend asked on the phone. We were chatting as I finished up day five of quarantine.

"Yes," I said. "Advil Cold and Flu Severe is the best, it takes away your body aches. Mucinex when you start to cough. And then, when you get a little hot and feverish at night, I like to eat some arugula in a small bowl with chopped cucumbers to cool down." I started to laugh. "Oops," I said, "this is 'The Idiot's Guide.'"

I went on. "Coconut water by the box. Every drink gets a reusable straw. So you drink more! Eat one less pickle than you think you should – the dehydrated morning vibe is atrocious. I also really liked the saline sprays like the one by Arm and Hammer and a humidifier. Just be sure to disinfect it regularly by running it with white vinegar. You'll lose your smell a little. You won't mind.

"Read books on the toilet. I like Sally Rooney. Make coffee and don't drink it. After four days of no makeup, realize it's a great time to start wearing a day cream. Then forget it. Oh and essential oil tablets that dissolve in the shower, I like eucalyptus. My mom sent these over as a treat. Have at least one conversation with someone who asks if you've used your Peloton during that free time at home. Throw up at night! Body aches by day! Fresh flowers in the baby's room! When your under-nose area gets red from blowing, and you're using chapstick anyway, put it under your nose too. When you finish the tissue box, stuff the new dirty tissues in it and voila! Tissue bin."

"What else?" My friend asked.

"Elmo," I said.

"For the kids, reusable sticker books, we have one of fish with ocean water background. Rest when the baby sleeps so you can keep up with her. Lay down paper towel magical paths. Put dolls to bed around the house. Unpack and repack boxes of coconut water. Don't leave the house for a week! Pink coil hair ties that your toddler can wear as a bracelet. Chicken broth in a sippy. Dinner at 4:57 p.m. Read books about excavators and other types of common diggers. Read one book in particular four times a day called I'm a Little Duck (twice at nap and twice before bed). That's the best book we have! Play baby shark, go crazy!

"Hold hands and sway while singing the ABCs. And when you get over your symptoms, don't go for an hour walk 'to look at the pup pups' like I did and then have to Google why am I so tired. Expect fatigue to swoop in after the sniffles dry up. Don't take off your jammies yet! This is quarantine. Did we even change our underwear? Try new socks. Deodorant? FaceTime your mom every day, sometimes so many times a day that she isn't possibly always available. Text everyone you're turning a corner one day before you are sure but 'you sense it coming.' Cross out every day of quarantine until you have 10 Xs on your wall calendar to match a weekend worth of canceled plans. Check daily to see what day it is and oops I still have five days left..."

Water With Ice

You know what is glamorous? Water with ice. Stockings with French dots. Double doors. Tall bookshelves. Fireplaces with photos on the mantle. The case of a lipstick. A watering can. A sun hat with a black ribbon.

But you know what is glamorous too? Sitting in the grass in the summer, blowing dandelions. Holding hands with your daughter walking barefoot wearing dresses. Pool hair at dinner. Corn on the cob cooked over the grill. A rocking chair brought down from the attic. Bonfires. Watching for shooting stars. Listening to crickets. A whole field of fireflies. Starting a playlist from memories. Swimming in the night. Swimming in the rain. Just family tonight. No glamor, thanks. Water with ice.

The Baby Is Two Now and So How Are We Doing?

Well, we have a harmonica named Monica that lives under the couch.

And sometimes I eat lunch under a blanket in bed. A few times, I've gone down the indoor toddler slide while she pushed. A few times.

Once, she told me, "Mama, I see fox," but it was a long-haired city dog she pointed to out the window.

She thought my parents' gray kittens were squirrels. She started a rumor that her grandparents "have goats."

I'm still not divorced two years into divorcing, which is the same length as my marriage. My child was unvaccinated for the majority of the global pandemic.

But you know what? Between the two of us, we've only had Covid three times.

Yesterday she came home with both legs in one side of her pants. Today someone wished me Happy Father's Day.

Not My Story Anymore

Today was S–'s last day of divorce group, and I dare say she didn't leave, she graduated.

Joe Dispenza says no one changes until they change their energy.

In time with grace, I too will say,

Not my story anymore!

PART TWO

♥

STRENGTH, HOPE & HEALING

A Letter from Marianna

Welcome, fellow divorcing friend, I see you, I am you. I promised myself in the darkness of my days through divorce that if I can share just one tidbit that helps another woman, even in the smallest of ways, during her journey, then my experience these past three years will not have been all for naught. This is a compilation of everything I would tell my best friend if she were going through divorce, written from my bedroom in downtown Boston and published to get into the hands of whoever may need it.

I remember thinking when I got married that, worst-case scenario, I could get divorced. Well, yes, but boy, was I misled in terms of the effects of trauma and upheaval it would have on my life. Many of us later admit to some extent we knew there were already troubles in our relationships, but we wanted so badly for them to work.

Even the most "gentle" divorce, with mediation, respectful co-parenting, and solid boundaries, is a major drastic life change and overhaul of your home, romantic, and financial life. It's a change in your identity, your finances, your home life, often your actual home, sometimes your job. The toll divorce takes on your heart is life-changing. Never mind the transition and rude awakening to becoming a single parent, where you might often feel like there is more work than one person can possibly do, plus the loneliness.

I had a high-conflict divorce with a custody battle over my minor infant child from when she was two months old to nearly three years – during the height of the pandemic. Lord, have mercy.

It has been a dark and lonely road.

On Finding the Words

In the beginning of my divorce, I did not know what had gone wrong in my marriage. I just knew I was banging my head against the wall trying to get through to him. Every conversation was a dead end, more confusing than the last. It made my head spin. I had never been at a loss for words like this. It was like I didn't have the terminology to express the emotional concepts. So I felt confused, of course. I could only cry. I couldn't speak. I was a snow globe of emotion I was trying not to shake.

The psychological understanding came later. What a relief to finally have the language (read: actually physiological terms) to express the complicated emotional concepts and why the fights in my marriage had all led to dead ends, also to take a deep dive into my own psychology and how I played a part in the unhealthy relationship from various psychological perspectives. I think it is important to take my own personal accountability here. It takes two to tango. I did not have half the emotional and psychological awareness that I do now.

On Still Healing

I write this now that I'm newly divorced. This writing has been a part of my healing journey for the past three years. I have considered waiting to write about it until I have "it all figured out" or at least more processed emotionally. But I have chosen instead to present my story and resources now, as a heal-ING individual, because I think that is more relatable. If I learn more, I will write more. And you can see how the time capsules of emotion are captured from all the different stages of grief. I am in a different place now than two or three years ago when much of this was written. I have accepted and I have let go. I still feel sadness and anger and grief and loneliness and more, and also, I know there was no other way. And my daughter is the greatest gift of all.

On Hurting

I posted a TikTok that being newly divorced feels like... you got on a surprise airplane, and landed in a surprise country, and you have to figure out where you are. The language, your new identity, home, work, everything feels new. Someone commented on the video (my first troll comment, I guess), "Good for you that your divorce feels like a vacation, some would say it's more like a tragic car crash." Oh dear, I thought. That's not what I meant at all. "No vacation here," I replied. "But that metaphor also checks out."

When you are in deep pain, it can be blinding. So to this person, and to those that also feel this way, I offer serious compassion because...

...I am a crash survivor too.

On How Slow the Process Moves

One of the hardest parts I found about divorce is the uncertainty, especially in regard to the timeframe. How long does it take to get divorced? I had no idea how long it would take. For some, it's quick – a year? Two years is possible when there's a young child. Covid slowed down the courts. Add a little conflict, custody, an emergency court motion, and yeah, the process slows. All I wanted was to rebuild my life. But I had to wait almost three years. So instead, I researched every day to stay hopeful of what my life could be and laid low in survival mode. I frequently stayed home for the past few years due to Covid isolation. And I had an infant. But I was also traumatized and afraid to make any sudden moves, afraid to "put my neck out."

It's only recently that I chose to be fearless.

When the divorce ended, I was basically in disbelief. I had just learned to live in survival mode (which is no way to live long-term). I was giddy for like two weeks after I got divorced. I was in such shock that the chains had lifted. But I needed a lot of grounding, meditation, gym time, social contact, therapy, grace and rest. And I still do. It's ongoing, this personal healing.

On Sitting Out the Storm

As women and mothers, we want to take care of everyone and everything. We are socially conditioned to be givers and selfless. I actually dislike the metaphor about putting the airplane mask on yourself first before your child. What if the child needs you first? That is what being a single mother of an infant felt like to me anyway – no time for myself to even pee when the baby needs me. Like you have to steal your self-care. I do get the airplane mask metaphor, by the way. But having no time for your own basic care without backup, well, it's taxing.

In divorce, as a mother – we don't let the sky fall. And so we are catching the pieces as they come tumbling down. You cannot start to rebuild your metaphorical family home until your life stops crumbling. But there's no way to gauge when these pieces will stop falling apart, or how long your divorce will take. And it feels like it's no use to wait, and there's an urgency to repair and keep yourself and your family healthy and strong. You can't wait for it all to end. There's an urgency to repair all that you can but sometimes before you can rebuild, you have to sit out the storm. Just like you can't heal from trauma until you feel safe, get to safe land, a therapist pointed out to me.

On Timelines, Guilt & Overwhelm

A very hard factor is not knowing the length of time of this destruction. Family court and divorce is a slow legal process. Hearings can often be scheduled in court three months out from one another. Mine all were. You can have a pre-trial hearing, and then another one. I did. Preparing your finances is a daunting task.

And how does a mother go back to work after being out of work while raising her kids for years? Do you put "Stay at Home Mother" on your resume with bullet points like "time management," "great under pressure," "multitasking proficient." I did. Or how does a mom find work when she also needs to prioritize her child?

And there is always some form of guilt. For breaking up your family, for leaving, for the pain that is so hard to release even when you know you did the right thing and you would not trade your story for ANYTHING ELSE because you have your beautiful child, who is a blessing.

It feels overwhelming and hard because it IS overwhelming and hard. It is not the path anyone would choose.

I had a thought when I was alone in lockdown bathing my infant daughter before I had any helpers or support system. I thought to myself as I washed my beautiful infant baby – God would not have given me this angelic baby girl if I could not rise to the task. I felt this to my core. I had to rise to the task. And I knew I would.

Also, please keep this in mind – every divorce is on its own time frame, its own narrative, and we all enter the process with different awareness and different scenarios, different players. Please don't let my story dishearten you. Take from it like observing an older sister so you might not make the same mistakes. I had someone say to me, "Man, this makes me afraid to get married." This was my response: "Don't be. You have the inner knowledge enough to have the intelligence to stop a train like this before it happens. You can trust yourself."

On Warrior Initiation

Divorce feels at times like a dark night of the soul. Like the hero's journey of a woman going into the dark forest alone to fight off dragons and demons to emerge a warrior goddess. It is like a coming-of-age story. Or a challenge that makes you a knight, a warrior, it can feel at times like you are fighting off the darkness and becoming a warrior of the light. You will not come out of this experience the same person. So you will shed your skins and you will emerge only carrying with you what most matters. If you do not become bitter, whether you like it or not, if you rise to the occasion and take the call, you will become a forged-in-the-fire warrior woman.

On The Empowered Divorcee, Who Is She?

Joe Dispenza says, "No one changes until they change their energy." And in a weird way, I have observed many other women in my divorce support group seemingly out of the blue (though after a lot of deep inner work) one day just have that new radiant energy, that empowered glow, their voice back, the ability to move through the traffic, the logs of the dam open up. And they can get employment, they get their own home, they get their new divorcee bed frame, they emerge like a beautiful butterfly out of the cocoon of divorce, as suddenly as they had fallen into it. The cocoon phase is dark. The divorce and co-parenting navigation is still there but:

"Eventually the divorce becomes a smaller sliver of the pie than other parts of your life," Oona Metz my divorce support group leader once explained. This rings true.

On Being Stuck in the Middle of a Slow Divorce, Feeling Sad

But the slow middle of a divorce is like being stuck in heavy traffic when you want to be getting somewhere on time. It can feel very sluggish and disheartening. I read, "Depression is anger you feel you are not allowed to have." Being in this cocoon or traffic state where you feel no one is hearing your voice or listening, and you have no control can lead to sluggishness and depression, anxiety, overwhelming heaviness. Thoughts like, "Why am I not moving faster?" "Why am I not making progress?" Don't lose hope. It's all just part of it. The gooey middle is where you do the deep work. And the deep work is where the magic happens. "Shut up," I can hear you thinking. Let me dial it back to what you might prefer to know:

What helps?

I have found "agency." Little accomplishments each day. Do the small things you can. Focus on what you do have control over. And gratitude. Make To-Do lists with easily accomplished tasks. Maybe the first one after "School Drop Off" is "A Short Walk In The Sun." I like the app Google Keep for my lists. Even if my lists are silly, I write them and I check them off. And I got through mad time this way.

Another thing Oona Metz said the other day is, "Sometimes it's not how fast you are moving but how deep."

Let's read that again:

"Sometimes it's not how fast you are moving in divorce through the legal process but how deep you are moving through the emotional arc."

Damn. It's not a fun process. But if you want to emerge an empowered warrior, a boundary badass, a beautiful butterfly, if you want to gain the psychological understanding and drop the trauma and move on with your life, you have to go really deep. And sometimes it's not a choice, sometimes the divorce just takes you on that wild ride.

Agency. Make a short, easy-to-accomplish list. And a gratitude list. Every day. Tag me. Trust me, you are not alone.

On Rebuilding Your Life

It truly is a warrior initiation. Because you cannot go through this experience and remain unchanged. So in a way, your old self dies too. I died on a few levels, if I'm being honest. My pre-mother self, my wife self with that married last name, my pre-Covid self, they're dead and gone. And who am I now? Marianna Saltonstall Pease. Who I was always going to be.

When you rebuild your life, I basically realized you're not starting from scratch. You're starting from who you always were, BUT at your most courageous, who you are at your core, and what you might have wished your life to look like as a child. Follow that. The pieces are all there; you just have to find a way for them to all fit together again, the hardest task.

I remember saying I don't know who I am anymore and realizing I'm the same. I don't know how to rebuild my life, but it was all the same pieces of my core I just had to rework. Everything's the same but the duo.

On Making Progress

"There is a legal and an emotional arc to divorce," Oona Metz says. And these arcs are not fast, and they are not linear.

Sometimes people can get frustrated because they don't know if they are making progress. They don't know what is up or down, or where they are in their journey, and when the trauma of the falling roof will end. Oona drew a line that led to a squiggly mess and then a line. The healing and the movement is a squiggle, not a straight line. This helped a few of us to get it.

Learning how to say aloud your "narrative" (how you tell your story) and having the support of a trusted therapist or friend to remind you of your progress is immeasurably helpful.

On Your New Life, Fake It 'til You Make It

When you start to emerge, with new energy, you may feel able to plan a solo trip, you may finally find employment that works for you as a single mom. You may start to date, or find a new partner who is radically different from your ex because they are kind and respect you, and they do not follow those previous unhealthy patterns of blaming, not hearing, forcing you to do things you don't feel comfortable with, etc. It might feel really foreign. You might resist it, or you might allow yourself to feel really seen. You might feel like you're practicing your boundaries, your new empowered self, but it won't feel perfect. Like how being an adult is still the same you as when you were younger, just with more responsibilities and wisdom, just like you are still you even if you fly to the other side of the world – you have to gain your footing and practice your boundaries daily, and maybe you will be dealing with co-parenting, a parenting schedule, the dynamics of your custody arrangements and looking out for your child's needs through the divorce. It is said, "At every level there is a new devil." When you come out of your divorce, it won't be easy, you'll still have challenges, but you will have the tools to handle them without panic. You've come this far, so honestly, what can't you handle? It comes down to trust and self-respect.

On Who Left Whom

Another tidbit for the middle of divorce – Oona Metz says, "There is often someone who ends the marriage and someone who leaves." The person that chooses the separation or to leave often gets the shit end of the stick, a lot of blame and anger towards them, but why did they leave? Were they unheard for years? Were they neglected and ignored when they tried to connect or speak or voice concerns? Were they treated fairly or decently in the first place? Was the dynamic in the relationship even a healthy one to model for kids? Did they ever have a voice before they left as the final straw?

On Shame and Guilt

Another thing that comes up besides deep grief and mourning for the person you thought your ex was, the future you had planned, is shame. Shame and guilt are often experienced during this process. If you have them, do not think you are alone. Divorce is a complex intermingling of emotions, and many feelings at the same time can be true. I have found the more you can write about them in a journal and share these hard emotions, the less tightly you hold onto them, the freer you can start to feel. Almost everyone will actually resonate with these themes in some way, and sharing is cathartic. The shame, guilt, and fear we hold the tightest in secrecy are often the most humanizing and relatable, and sharing your burden can lessen it. Being a human is hard. Life is wildly complicated. If you have guilt or shame, my main suggestion is to journal and find openings to talk to someone. Possibly only you are the most upset about it. Possibly if a dear friend heard, they'd be like, "Yeah, that's real," and hug you through your tears. Deep breath, sister!

On Loneliness

"It is better to be alone than in bad company."
– George Washington

You will not be alone forever unless you choose to be. You are only broken or "damaged goods" if you decide to be. Truly. If you don't allow yourself to be hardened, if you believe in your self-worth, and that there is happiness and someone out there for you, there is. You're only mostly limited here by your own self-belief.

"What is for me shall not pass me."
– Unknown

On Dating Again

That being said, during the deep healing stage of your divorce, it may be better to be single. Let me explain. You have to become aware of old dating patterns so you can break them and form new healthier ways. You need to bump up your self-worth and your boundaries, your standards, and rebuild your life so that you attract the right new partner. So don't feel pressure to rush to date. If you date before you are healed, it is much easier to, even if you think you won't, attract the old kind of mate, the unhealthy patterns will play out again, you will fall into your old habit of codependency or attracting a narcissist, or poor boundaries, or people pleasing or getting love bombed, or jumping in too soon, or blurring (ignoring) red flags. If you haven't pumped up your self-worth, you will maybe accept breadcrumbs from a romantic partner instead of being treated the way you would treat your own friends, with respect and kindness.

If you have to wonder if he likes you, if he's ever going to text, if he wants to see you again, if he truly likes you for you rather than just something physical, if he will ever change, if it's a red flag, girl, run. There is more for you.

If it's good but you feel in your gut it's not aligned for the true you. Don't settle.

If you see a red flag and you make an excuse. I call this "blurring a red flag." If you blur a red flag by making excuses, what you are doing, girl, is PURPOSELY IGNORING A RED FLAG. And we know what's gonna happen long term now. Don't follow old patterns.

There is a saying, "This or something better."

Life coach Cara Alwill says,

"Your self-respect has to always be stronger than your emotions."

"When you abandon your boundaries, you abandon yourself."

Or how about this Instagram meme:

"I will be single until a man says he cannot breathe without me."

On the Ending of Divorce

When you near the end of your divorce, it may feel like a plane coming in for a landing with some turbulence as you brace your seat and prepare for the new country you landed in.

On Valentines Day 2023, my divorce support group met in person. One woman came in with a cardboard box filled with river stones she had collected that were all the shape of hearts. Some tiny thin pebbles, some big fat hearts. We each choose one to keep on our desk, our kitchen sill, or in our pocket for divorce hearings. Then she pulled out of her bag something else. Photos of some graffiti she had seen on a walk, she had printed them and it read: Refuse to Shrink. I went home with my divorce bounty and I put that postcard up on my wall. It remains there.

You may feel at the end of your divorce like you are becoming unfrozen. Like you had been walking through life in a type of survival mode, like a bubble head, a little floaty. I believe that is a psychological protection for your nervous system called dissociation. It's to protect you when it's all too much. As you unfreeze, you will feel freer and happier. But what would you tell your frozen self to cope with? How would you tell that scared and hopeless version of yourself how to spend their time? Long walks, be easy on yourself, practice breathing, calm activities, self-compassion. See my ABCs of Self-Care coming up.

On Courage

I was walking past a construction site during my divorce and I found a small rock that someone had written on in pen: "Pressure makes diamonds."

You are a diamond. No, you are a strong, courageous, empowered woman in the making and there is nothing more beautiful than being called to a great challenge. You will feel there is no way in hell you can accomplish such a giant task – but, "You have survived everything in your life this far," Cara Alwill says, and as my mother says, "There is no end to how strong you have to be." You will be a different person on the other side – which is scary – the death, in a way, of your old self. But the badass that will emerge is the warrior woman that you need to be. Show the example, and model this strength and empowerment for your children.

It takes courage to divorce. It takes courage to step out of an unhealthy and unhappy relationship dynamic. It is not for the small or weak. But the rewards are you get your life back and you get to live as your true self. Be brave. There is nothing more beautiful than a courageous woman. And there is always dawn after the darkness.

It is NOT easy to get out of these hard (toxic, abusive, love-absent, demeaning or soul-sucking) relationships, especially when we have built our lives around them with young children involved. Also, if you have spent years in a toxic or hardening environment, slowly and continually losing aspects of yourself, giving your power away, and now you feel lost yourself – like "Who am I anymore?" – I understand this too. Sometimes it takes a long time to work up the bravery to take your life back. And sometimes the right time for your children is later. And sometimes it's an actually terrifying situation and you need to find help to get out. But there is help. There is help if you need it. I have listed concrete resources at the back of this book. If you are in a dangerous situation, my prayers go out to you. Please know you are worthy, as Heather Havrilesky says, "The question of your worthiness is not even on the table." Your dreams are enough.

As I was driving home one day, I heard on the radio the line, "Not my story anymore." And I want to share this with you because divorce, though seemingly infinite, does end. And the trauma you have gone through can be healed. You will be a bolder and brighter version of yourself from what you have gone through. Divorce is an opportunity, if you let it be, for tremendously deep healing, redirection, and, as I like to call it, "a bonus life."

With love and good wishes for your bonus life to arrive perfectly soon,

Marianna

The Stages of Grief

I find it helpful to know about the stages of grief because I totally thought I could maybe skip a step and hopefully move through them faster. Yeah right! (Also, does everyone think that? Or just me?) They are telltale steps for a reason. But I like having concrete ways to frame my emotions which can feel amorphous without the terms to understand them, so this helped me. Maybe it will help you. Otherwise, don't worry about them, and disregard them. Take a deep breath, and now you can read them:

1. **Denial** (This is NOT happening to me!)
2. **Anger** (WTF is this happening to me!)
3. **Bargaining** (Maybe if I did this, or I should have done that, or if I try this, the outcome could be different.)
4. **Depression** (This sucks, where is my control? I am sad, I have anger, I have nowhere to direct it.)
5. **Acceptance** (This happened. But it does not define me and I will not let it hold me back. In a way, it may be a blessing in disguise.)

Box Breath

If you experience strong anxiety or panic attacks (which can feel like a burning feeling in your chest if your heart rate elevates), I have learned that if I take deep breaths, I can control my heart rate and slow down my anxiety, and this helps me find comfort.

Mentally repeat to yourself: I AM SAFE. Put your hand over your heart. It might be too scary to come to the present moment, or you may resist wanting to be still in your body, but that's okay, even one deep breath is a good deep breath. Other things I like for anxiety before bed: a sleep mask, lavender and chamomile essential oil, tea, cozy pajamas, a weighted blanket, a white noise machine. And see next page.

The Box Breath to soothe the nervous system:

>**Inhale to the count of 4**
>
>**Hold your breath for the count of 4**
>
>**Exhale for the count of 4**
>
>**Hold breath to the count of 4**

Bedtime Ritual

In the evening before you go to bed, lie with your feet up the wall on your bed and listen to calming music on headphones or a meditation app. This helps to stop ruminating before sleep. I read a quote that said, "Worrying is like praying for what you do not want." Whether or not you are spiritual, it has helped me a lot to take my worries and hand them over to a higher power or imagine putting them aside in a box so that you can rest. My mother says, "You have done all that you can do in a day."

This pose is great for lymphatic drainage, increasing circulation, getting off your feet if you've been running around all day, and creating a calm space before bed.

If this sounds to you like total shit, you can create any bedtime ritual, even for five minutes, that creates a safe place for you to switch off your racing thoughts. You could read fiction before bed and get lost in stories from other times and worlds. You could needlepoint and watch comedies or documentaries. You can order beautiful artistic paint-by-numbers kits off Etsy or color in an adult coloring book. The idea is to stop negative rumination before your sleep.

Breathwork and Guided Meditation

I realized I love guided meditations for helping me release stored emotions by visualizing them leaving. Being in your body can be scary if you have a lot of emotion, pain or trauma. I found guided meditations a really unique way to release my pain and grief for healing.

I love Studio Intune by Elevate the Globe and Evolve by Erika, app which both have free trials. I have found these breathing exercises to be very calming for my nervous system. I also love the Superhuman app and Calm.com. Spirit Mamas is a beautiful woman-led group of energy workers I highly recommend which has amazing guided meditations for somatic healing and one on one sessions.

YouTube also has great free meditation and affirmation videos. My favorite affirmation YouTube video is *Be Free Butterfly* by Tony Samara, which can be viewed here:

https://www.youtube.com/watch?v=rUID23p03Q8

A Card a Day

In college, a hippy friend of mine told me I would probably love angel cards. Boy, do I. My college roommate and I kept them on the kitchen counter in a little dish and I still like to pick one a day and leave it on the kitchen counter. You can ask a question first or just choose for the day. They say things like "inspiration," "healing," "intention," "release," and I find them to be perfectly timed and a fun way to tap into my emotions and inner voice. If I get too "heady" and overthinking everything, they can bring me back to an essence.

You can do the same thing with oracle cards or tarot cards.

I created my own deck of affirmations for healing based on what I've been through, the *I Make My Own Luck* affirmation card deck, which is available for purchase online and at www.oonascollection.com I created it as a sister project to this book.

Affirmations

Here is a small sampling of a few of my favorite affirmations. I have worked with an amazing graphic designer, Chantelle Davis Gray, to design my card deck that is available for purchase at www.oonascollection.com. Below are a few of my favorites.

>When you abandon your boundaries, you abandon yourself.
>
>Barn burned down, now I can see the moon.
>
>Do something today your future self will thank you for.
>
>Rejection is divine redirection.
>
>I trust the divine timing of my life.
>
>What is for me shall not pass me.
>
>What is coming is better than what has gone.
>
>Your self-respect has to be stronger than your emotions.
>
>I let go of what is no longer in alignment.
>
>What would my most empowered self do?

The Serenity Prayer

God, grant me the serenity to accept the things I cannot change,

courage to change the things I can,

and wisdom to know the difference.

Psalm 23

The Lord is my shepherd; I shall not want.

He maketh me to lie down in green pastures: he leadeth me beside the still waters.

He restoreth my soul: he leadeth me in the paths of righteousness for his name's sake.

Yea, though I walk through the valley of the shadow of death, I will fear no evil: for thou art with me; thy rod and thy staff, they comfort me.

Thou preparest a table before me in the presence of mine enemies: thou anointest my head with oil; my cup runneth over.

Surely goodness and mercy shall follow me all the days of my life: and I will dwell in the house of the Lord forever.

Quotations

"And the day came when the risk to remain tight in a bud was more painful than the risk it took to blossom."

– Anais Nin

"I come in peace, but I mean business."

– Janelle Monae

"Look, you live one life. Give it all you lipping got and take all your shots. One's bound to hit the target."

– Harnaam Kaur

"When you're in your lane, there's no traffic."

– Ava Duvernay

"Fear is boring."

– Elizabeth Gilbert

"Stay afraid, but do it anyway."

– Carrie Fisher

"Be bold. Envision yourself living a life that you love."

– Suzan-Lori Parks

"It's amazing what we can do if we simply refuse to give up."

– Octavia Butler

"The question of your worthiness is not on the table at all."

– Heather Havrilesky

"There's a crack in everything. That's how the light gets in."

– Leonard Cohen

"Strong women don't have 'attitudes,' we have standards."

– Marilyn Monroe

"Always be a first-rate version of yourself, instead of a second-rate version of somebody else."

– Judy Garland

"Above all, be the heroine of your life, not the victim."

– Nora Ephron

"Stay strong. Stand up. Have a voice."

– Shawn Johnson

"A strong woman knows she has strength enough for the journey, but a woman of strength knows it is in the journey where she will become strong."

    – Unknown

"A really strong woman accepts the war she went through and is ennobled by her scars."

    – Carly Simon

"Women are like teabags. We don't know our true strength until we are in hot water."

    – Eleanor Roosevelt

Psychological Glossary

First off, I am not a therapist or formally trained in any sort of psychology unless you count my first year of psychology graduate school that I completed, which has now manifested in a massive interest, but let's not. I am merely a layperson who finds the language of psychological understanding empowering, as it allows you to put words and concepts to what is otherwise an amorphous feeling.

That being said, I don't feel I am at liberty to best explain these topics, but rather I will present them in my own words as a first introduction so that if they resonate, you may do your own research or bring them to the attention of your own therapist.

A note on labels. Labels are often limiting, not the whole picture, and usually dehumanizing when placed on people. I try not to refer to a person as a label. But identifying these traits is also a helpful way to frame understanding behavior. But I want to mention this as a slippery line to walk, to talk about labels to understand behavior but try to refrain from limiting people.

I highly recommend working with a therapist or being in a support group during any kind of life transition or trauma, such as divorce, because of the emotional support and the practical guidance and the sisterhood that come from the shared experience.

If you don't know where to begin in looking for a therapist or a support group, you can start with the list of support groups and resources at the back of this book.

Anyways, relationships break up, and a lot of people get divorced, but if you want to take a DEEPER look at WHY instead of just pointing the finger, check out the psychological glossary.

Psychology Resource: Another amazing resource is Dr. Nicole LePera. The Holistic Psychology on Instagram is another incredible resource. She also has a book called *How to Do the Work*.

Trauma Responses

Fight ("Attack" mode to ensure one's safety)

Flight ("Run away" mode to ensure one's safety)

Freeze ("Can't move, immobilized" mode of action for safety)

Fawn (Hyper-people pleasing to try to ensure your own safety)

Trauma Trigger

Anything that reminds you of a past time you did not feel safe and makes you feel similarly now. See Trauma Responses.

Boundaries

"This is your reminder that the boundaries you set are meant for you, not others' behavior." – Terrie Vanover

Learning to set boundaries is a skill. It is like building muscle. If you are not used to setting boundaries, you might feel "mean" at first. But truthfully, everyone benefits from clear communication. Always.

And people respect those who communicate their needs and wants clearly. You will disappoint 100 times more if you aim to please and then retract.

From the start, try to look within at what you need and reply from your inner voice: Does this serve me? Listening and acting on your gut is a superpower. It is freedom. Be your own parent.

Codependency

Codependency is expecting your partner to fulfill your emotional and physical needs instead of filling your own cup. Relying on others for your needs overly heavily.

Does your love feel like an addiction? Were you abandoned in childhood, either literally or emotionally, and so you are seeking to heal this in your adult romantic relationships by filling the void by over-loving those emotionally inconsistent or only offering you breadcrumbs, not meeting you halfway? There is an AA for co-dependents because it really can feel like a love addiction. See: CoDA.org, Co-Dependents Anonymous.

People Pleasing

Abandoning yourself for the sake of others. Technically a type of passive way to try to control. Causes resentment and a complete abandonment of your own needs and lack of boundaries.

Go really deep as to why you have this learned behavior. This often stems from childhood attachment or how you navigated your early days in your family system. What was your role in your family? Were you expected to take care of everyone? Did you need to be nice? Is this method of learned behavior still serving you in your adult life? How can you look better out for ME? See: Boundaries.

Attachment Theory

Bowdy and Ainsworth are psychologists who studied childhood attachment. Some believe that adults recreate these early attachment styles in their adult relationships which can be troubling if the relationships are unhealthy and the parties are unaware of them.

If you felt abandoned in childhood, are you seeking out emotionally unavailable partners in hopes this time they won't abandon you? But they still do?

Are you looking for a mother or father figure figuratively in your partner that will save you instead of taking full accountability for your own life?

Everyone is fully accountable for their own life, which also means the results of it. You can't point the finger and blame. It's on you to make something of your life.

Are you seeking the love and approval you didn't have growing up? Your partner is not responsible for your happiness or caring for you because you dropped the ball on personal responsibility.

> **Ambivalent Attachment** (Distressed when parent leaves, cannot depend on parent to be there)
>
> **Disorganized Attachment** (Inconsistent)
>
> **Avoidant Attachment** (Avoid caregiver not attached)
>
> **Secure Attachment** (Happy confident)

Learn more at:
https://www.simplypsychology.org/attachment.html

Narcissism

I always thought a narcissist was a vain person. Oh no. It's deeper. It's a personality type where the individual feels no empathy and is very focused on image, among other things.

If you want to learn about narcissism, there is a great resource on YouTube. Search Doctor Ramani and narcissism on YouTube and she very well explains it. Things like gaslighting, smear campaigns, lack of empathy and tactics. Information is power.

In fact, there is a whole slew of terms that can help make a lot of sense out of your situation if this is at play:

> **Love bombing:** Building you up, making you feel overly special, especially too early in dating
>
> **Supply:** Feeding off the benefit of being around/with something for their image
>
> **Flying Monkeys:** Abuse by proxy, the people the narcissist employs to work with them
>
> **Word Salad:** Jumble of words, crazy-making, meant to deflect accountability by confusion
>
> **Devaluation:** When the narcissist can no longer use you for supply, you are discarded

**"People don't abandon people they love-
they abandon people they were using." -Unknown**

> **Smear Campaign:** Trying to take you down as a person, making themselves the victim, torturing you as revenge or to get what they want, revenge
>
> **Lack of Empathy:** Do they not care if you cry? Never apologize or take responsibility, shift the blame. Most people care if they hurt you.

Blaming/No Responsibility: A narcissist will NEVER take responsibility; everything will always and forever be your fault. This will never change, you will never be able to explain.

D.A.R.V.O

A technique used to manipulate reality in high-conflict toxic relationship situations. Creepy! Stands for:

Deny
Attack
Reverse Victim and
Offender

Dissociation

When you feel frozen or bubble-headed or spacey. The nervous system's way of shutting down to protect you from trauma or a moment that triggers you because it feels like the past and is a system overload, too much.

What helps? Wiggle your fingers and toes. Five senses. Ground in your reality. Deep breaths. Self-care. Don't make big decisions or take big actions. Therapy. Healing work. Go slow.

Gaslighting

Some concrete examples of gaslighting:

> I don't understand.
> I never did that.
> That never happened.
> I was just kidding.
> I never said that.
> You sound crazy. You're crazy.
> I'm so worried about you.
> You need help.
> If I'm so bad, why are you with me?

Emotional Abuse

When you are controlled and have no voice and are led to feel crazy or fearful and powerless. You can slip into it and not realize because it happens slowly, little by little, and you give your power away over time. A scary term to throw around but important to have awareness of how it happens and what it entails.

Some Concrete examples of emotional abuse:

> Blaming
> Shaming
> Poking fun
> Insults
> Rejection
> Silent treatment – as a tactic for control
> Gaslighting

Devaluation

Smear campaign

Humiliating

Scapegoating

Insults masked as jokes

Isolating you from friends and family physically or your communication

Extreme controlling jealousy

Unpredictable angry outbursts

Blame shifting, never taking responsibility

Name calling

Withholding affection

How do we end up in a toxic or emotionally abusive or unhealthy relationship?

How do we give our power away? We give our power away little by little. By people pleasing, by fawning, but not being aware of our attachment styles and family dynamics from childhood. By giving your power away little by little, you can lose your power and be in an unhealthy relationship dynamic and not even know.

Just like we give our power away little by little over time, we have to regain our power little by little, which takes time. Like the stage of grief, this process cannot be rushed. You have to give yourself time to heal, and plenty of grace.

Physical Abuse

*Physical abuse: Physical harm caused intentionally

"Physical abuse is intentional bodily injury. Some examples include slapping, pinching, choking, kicking, shoving, or inappropriately using drugs or physical restraints. Signs of physical abuse." – From WA.gov

Please see resources at the back of this book. Help is available.

Coercive Control

Subtle control by an abusive partner.

Some examples: Isolation from friends and family, isolation from getting help, always speaking or seeing family and friends with your partner on speakerphone or with you so you cannot get out. Prior to this is love bombing making you feel like the best ever and then sometimes followed by financial manipulation.

Reactive Abuse

Pushing someone's buttons subtly but incessantly until they snap – then blame deflecting to point your finger at how they snapped as "the issue."

On Therapy

First and foremost, I strongly encourage those who are doing deep emotional healing to see a therapist, join a support group or seek mental health support of some kind. Family and friends can become overburdened and finding your support systems is not just beneficial but a crucial lifeline in the healing process.

On Healthy Lifestyle and Medication

Additionally, I want to mention that diet, exercise and a healthy lifestyle really helps in the healing process. I strongly recommend joining a gym, running, or at least walking.

Taking vitamins like vitamin D is commonly accepted, so why not take a medication like an antidepressant or anti-anxiety medication during a difficult period in your life if it is apt to help you get through it? Many people are against the idea of trying medication, and I have been there, but I believe that anything that can help get someone during a traumatic season of their life successfully and gracefully over the hump is worthwhile. That's my plug for mental health awareness. Remember, you do not need to suffer and if there is help, why not take it? If you have come as far as you can on your own and you are still suffering, seek out additional help. There are many resources available for those who seek them.

    Massage (good for removing trauma in the body)
    Pilates (good for strength, endurance and mental health)
    Walking (with a good podcast in the sun)
    Acupuncture (for healing)
    Breathwork Mediations (for calming the nervous system)
    Yoga (great for healing and practicing self-compassion)
    Tapping, EFT ("Emotional freedom technique)
    Sunbathing
    Biking
    Dancing
    Rockclimbing
    Individual Therapy

Support groups

Group therapy

Nature

Family

Spirituality

Friends

Pets

Art

Music

Dancing

Sports

Rest

Reading

Pandemic Mom Book Club / Recommended Reading List:

1. *The Kickass Single Mom: Be Financially Independent, Discover Your Sexiest Self, and Raise Fabulous, Happy Children* by Emma Johnson

2. *The Book of Boundaries: Set The Limits That Will Set You Free* by Melissa Urban

3. *The Places That Scare You: A Guide to Fearlessness In Difficult Times* by Pema Chodron

4. *The Four Agreements* by Don Miguel Ruiz

5. *Available: A Memoir of Sex And Dating After A Marriage Ends* by Laura Friedman Williams

6. *Divorcing and Healing From A Narcissist: Emotional and Narcissistic Abuse Recovery. Co-Parenting after an Emotionally Destructive Marriage and Splitting up with a Toxic Ex* by Dr. Theresa J. Covert

7. *BIFF For Co-Parent Communication: Your Guide to Difficult Co-Parent Texts, Emails, and Social Media Posts* by Bill Eddy, LCSW, ESQ. Annette T. Burns, JD and Kevin Chafin, LPC

8. *Trauma and Recovery: The Aftermath of Violence – From Domestic Abuse to Political Terror* by Judith Herman, MD

9. *The Empowered Woman's Guide to Divorce: A Therapist and a Lawyer Guide you Through Your Divorce Journey* by Jill A. Murray, PsyD, Adam R. Dodge, JD

10. *Warrior Goddess Training: Become the Woman You Are Meant to Be* by Heatherash Amara

11. *The Power is Within You* by Louise Hay

12. *You Can Heal Your Life* by Louise Hay

13. *How To Do the Work: Recognize Your Patterns, Heal from Your Past and Create Your Self* by Dr. Nicole Lepera, The Holistic Psychologist

14. *The Body Keeps the Score: Brain, Mind, and Body in the Healing of Trauma* by Bessel Van Der Kolk, M. D.

15. *The Inner Gym: A 30-Day Workout for Strengthening Happiness* by Light Watkins

16. *Healing Through Words* by Rupi Kaur

17. *Magnetic Mindset: How to Make Love to the Universe and Manifest Anything* by Gala Darling

18. *Girl On Fire* by Cara Alwill

19. *Style Your Mind: A Workbook and Lifestyle Guide for Women Who Want to Design Their Thoughts, Empower Themselves and Build a Beautiful Life* by Cara Alwill

20. *IDK...yet: Choose What "Living Your Best Life" Looks Like and Create It* by The Manifesting Queen Jess Redfern

21. *The Depression Cure: The 6 Step Program to Beat Depression Without Drugs* by Stephen S. Ilardi

22. *The Narc Decoder: Understanding the Language of the Narcissist* by Tina Tina Swithin

23. *Recovery from Narcissistic Abuse, Gaslighting, Codependency, and Complex PTSD, 4 books in 1 Workbook and Guide to Overcome Trauma, Toxic Relationships, Anxiety, and Improve Mental Health* by Linda Hill

Music

Check out my Spotify account **Heypandemicmom** for my divorce healing playlists.

"F*** Divorce I'm Powerful Now: Empowered Healing Songs for the Bad Bitch"

https://open.spotify.com/playlist/3BRS147loEVLmKwvd3otIe

I also have a playlist for meditation here:

https://open.spotify.com/playlist/1TKYJVuJiZijg7xDJ8W7mG

Podcasts

One way to get info if you are afraid of having books lying around, especially if you are still living with your ex, is to go on walks and listen to podcasts (or audiobook downloads on your phone).

Single Mother Survival Guide
Divorced Not Dead by Caroline Stanbury
Solo Parent Life
Single Mom Nation
Solo Parent by AccessMore
We Can Do Hard Things
Out Of Crazy Town
The Narcissistic Trauma Recovery Podcast
One Mom's Battle
Style Your Mind by Cara Alwill
Move With Heart by MWH
Evolve By Erika
And She Rises by Amanda Frances
Gala Loves Everything by Gala Darling

Comedy

Mom and Divorce Comedy (For when you need some laughs)

    I Mom So Hard on YouTube, mom-friendly comedy
    Cat and Nat on YouTube, mom-friendly comedy
    Kat Stikler on IG and TikTok, divorced mom comedy
    Wine Country movie on Netflix
    Girlfriends Guide to Divorce TV series
    Single Parents TV series
    The Let-Down TV series, new moms

ABCs Of Self Care

Audiobooks, Acceptance, Art

Baths, Books, Breathwork, Budget

Cooking, Candles, Community, Crystals

Declutter your space

Exercise, EFT (Emotional Freedom Technique)

Fresh flowers, Farmers Market, Family, Friends

Get active, Guided meditation, Gratitude lists, Give back to others, Games

Hugs, Headphones and a podcast on a walk, Haircut

Intuition, Inner voice

Jogging

Keeping the faith, Knowing you are safe, Knowing you are strong and worthy of your dreams

Light (open the windows, light a candle, get your Vitamin D)

Manicure, Music, Massage, Meditation

Nourishing meals, Nice smelling body lotion, Needlepoint, Nature time, saying No

Open the windows, Organize

Pilates, Plants, Pedicure, Podcasts, Pets, Pray, Paint

Quiet time

Rest, Reading, Rockclimbing

Singing, Sunlight, Support groups, Spirituality, Swimming, Skincare, Sauna

Travel, Therapy

Unconditional Self-Love

Videos that are uplifting on YouTube or Netflix

Walks, Weighted blanket

X…Don't call your ex!

Yoga

Zzzs

Fun Self-Care Tips

Sleep in the middle of your bed. A year into my divorce, I realized I was still sleeping on "my side" without thinking about it. WTF? So, I moved the bed in the room so that his side was magically gone and started sleeping in the middle. Later I got my own new bed frame and new matching bedside tables to put books on either one! Delightful!

> **Take salt baths and read poetry**
> **Move your furniture to change the energy**
> **Put a sun catcher in the window**
> **Collect heart-shaped rocks by a river**
> **Get a semi-permanent fake tattoo** (Inkbox.com)
> **Get a chunky divorce ring from going thrifting.** Married to yourself!
> **Pour your coffee into a thrifted cool cup**
> **Try a new hobby.**

In my divorce, there was a week where two different people said to me, "You don't have any hobbies," and I was like, I mean, I have a kid, how am I supposed to do that? But the truth was I didn't.

And I think that as I have explored hobbies, I realized that you don't have to stick to one forever; you can sample them out for a few months. Physical hobbies have been really healing for me, but creative hobbies are also a great outlet. There are lots of continuing adult education places often in the cities you can join or on Zoom.

A short list of hobbies: to inspire if you don't know where to start. I would say that if there was something you tried as a kid and loved but never pursued as an adult, it's great to pick back up. If your child has an overnight at their other parent's, it's a great activity to sign up for a class at a center for both the social company and to learn your new skill.

- Rockclimbing gym
- Pilates classes
- Writing classes
- Painting classes
- Ceramics class
- Hiking day trip (there are groups for singles that like to hike on Facebook – same for rock climbing and skiing)
- Skiing
- Dancing lessons
- Singing lessons or chorus
- Musical instrument
- Reading before bed and getting a Kindle (makes you more interesting to talk to!)
- Gardening
- Sauna/Steam room
- Needlepoint
- Painting
- Cooking
- Flower arranging
- Etsy has artisan paint-by-number kits you can make as gifts
- Learn a new language on the Duolingo app and plan to travel there after your divorce is finalized

JOURNALING ♥ PROMPTS

In addition to therapy, support groups and calling friends, journaling is very beneficial for finding out the truth of how you feel and think and what your inner self knows you need and to be true.

Let's give it a go.

I am: (Write full name. Maiden Name)

Who am I? (Mother, Sister, Religion, Profession, Location, Politics, Beliefs, Values, Missions, Joys, Achievements, Dreams, Wishes, Visions)

When I was a child what did I love?

What did I want for my life as a child?

Do I still want any of that?

Would my young self be proud of me?

What do I need to still do to make her proIn what ways can I be kinder to myself?

If my best friend or loved one was speaking to me, what would they say? What advice do people offer me that is good for me to hear?

Going through the darkest times, but knowing my future self will emerge, what will I name my post-divorce alter ego?

What does she look like?
How does she feel?
What does she do for fun?
How does she celebrate her divorce?
How does she rebuild her life?
How does she get her power back?
What does her power look like? In what forms? Think big.

What makes me feel calm and safe? Think of the five senses. Do certain places, people, songs, foods, books, and feelings make me feel calm and safe? How can I give myself more of these calm feelings?

Who was I? Before the marriage, in the marriage?
Who will I be after?

Who is the ideal version of my future self that I am on my way to becoming? The fabulous divorcee – who is she? If you have NO IDEA, dream a little: what would be SO empowering?? Did your ex hate tennis and now you want to take a tennis lesson? Was he allergic to cats and now you might like to adopt a cat?

How can I help others with what I have been through?

Do I want to?

What would I do if I was BRAVE AND COURAGEOUS?

Where would I want to help people?

What kinds of people?

Where would I want to give back or volunteer or create that I didn't have?

What am I proud of myself for? List your proudest achievements, big and small:

What would I tell myself If I could reassure myself?

What am I sad about? How do I know? What makes me sad? How can I soothe myself for this? How can I love myself better through this sadness?

What am I angry about?

How does it present itself?

What do I do with my anger?

How might I better recognize it and release my anger?

Where in my body is my anger?

What does it look like?

What does it feel like?

Where can I put it if I were to release it?

In what areas do I have loosey-goosey or no boundaries?

Define a boundary you want to set.

How will you set it? How will that feel? And is that still worth it and why:

In what areas do I have good boundaries?

What are my strengths?

What do I want to work on?

What do I resist wanting to think about or admit to myself?

Who do I admire? Who are some of the coolest badass courageous individuals I know or have seen as celebrities?

What about them do I admire?

How can I emulate those qualities?

Who is the best evolved, highest version of myself?
What does she wear?
What does she do for work?
Where does she hang out?
What kinds of friends does she have?
Where does she live?
What is her partner like?
How does she speak to herself?
What is her morning routine?
Her evening routine?
What does she do before bed?
What time does she go to bed?

What am I grateful for? List everything that comes to mind:

How do I want to feel day to day in my new life?

What will I be grateful for when all of my dreams come true? Write down all of your greatest dreams in very specific details (use the five senses) as if they have already happened and express your gratitude for them.

♥

Organizations and Resources

For women who were abandoned by their partners:
Vikki Stark, Books, Empowerment, a whole movement
www.runawayhusbands.org

For women who were cheated on:
The Chump Lady, Blog, humor, a whole movement
www.chumplady.com

Narcissistic abuse support:
Dr. Ramani on YouTube

Tina Swithin of Onemomsjourney.com, Books, Support groups, Info PDFs

Tracey Malone of narcissticabusesupport.com

Domestic Violence Resources:
National Domestic Violence Hotline 800-799-7233

Text START to 88788

https://casamyrna.org/

https://www.domesticviolenceroundtable.org

Women's Divorce Support Groups:
Oona Metz, Divorce Support Therapy Groups, life changing group therapy, Oonametz.com

Jane Does Well, Divorce Support Groups and Community events, janedoeswell.org

SAS For Women, Divorce Coach Support Groups, Sasforwomen.com

Untied Untied.net, Divorce support groups NYC Based

New Moms Support:

JFSCboston.com and **JCC**, Support Groups for New Moms

Additional Support Groups and Resources:

Little Lovage Club

Peanut App – Has single mother groups

Facebook – Groups for divorce and single parents, home fix-it projects, and all sorts of support

Divorced Moms Healing – My Facebook group

HandyWomen Northeast – Facebook group

Boston Business Women's Group for Women entrepreneurs and directly for women owned services

Solo Parent Society

Christian Ministry with daily Zoom support groups for Christian solo parents

Soloparent.org

Huffington Post – Has a Divorce Section

Spirit Mamas – Victoria and Tiffany for energy healing, cutting the chords, inner voice work and womb healing

"You can cut all the flowers but you cannot stop Spring from coming."

– Pablo Neruda

Acknowledgments

Thank you from the bottom of my heart to my sisterhood: **Sophia J, Lily H., Esther B., Valentina V., Ilana L., Rachel Y.** for your patience and advice and love. How can I ever repay you? I love each of you like a real sister. Thank you for believing in me and being my soul sisters. And thank you, **Oona M.** I always joke you are doing god's work but truly believe that in the way you truly hold space for us to do the most transformational work we will do in our lives. **Amy B.** I have no words, only love and gratitude. Thank you. **S-, D-, B-, R-, N-, T-, A-**, and all who have touched me from your incredible honesty and vulnerability which carries so much power and strength. And for all the **Unseen Warrior Women** doing the work alone or in the dark, I see you, I am you and there is always light after the darkness. I write this for you. Thank you to **Victoria at Spirit Mamas**, for helping me find my power again. Thank you to the ladies at **Jane Does Well** for your heroic work. Thank you to **Yvonne** who led my new parent support group at **JFSC**. You are an angel. Thank you to the **midwives at Dartmouth Hitchcock hospital and the midwife who delivered A. and the woman who whispered in my ear during labor**, god bless you I could seriously cry. Thank you to **Yonabel** and **Sheli** I am so grateful to have you ladies in our life as amazing role models for my little daughter. Thank you to the **team at Unbound Press.** And, I would like to thank my **Mother and Father** always and forever. I love you both to the moon and back. I owe you both my deepest love and gratitude. To **Nat**, my bestie for 30 years. **To my daughter.** I loved you before you were born. I will love you forever. I love you all day. I love you all night.

Connect With Marianna:

Website: www.mariannapease.com

Blog: heypandemicmom.substack.com

Instagram @heypandemicmom

TikTok: @heypandemicmom

Twitter: @marianna108

YouTube: Hey Pandemic Mom

"Divorced Moms Healing" Facebook Group

Vintage Store: Instagram: @oonascollection

Online Store: www.oonascollection.com

I Make My Own Luck affirmation deck, available at www.mariannapease.com

About the Author

Marianna Saltonstall Pease is a divorced single mom by day and a writer by night. After going through a divorce while navigating the pandemic during new motherhood, she has written a book about her emotional healing in hopes to give back to others so they might have a guiding light or glimmer of hope. Additionally, she runs the longtime vintage clothing store www.oonascollection.com and writes the blog heypandemicmom.substack.com about her journey to emotional healing. She lives in Boston with her daughter.

Pandemic Mom is one part memoir, one part healing balm for the divorcing woman or new mama or any woman who finds herself in a dark night of the soul without a light. Part One covers Marianna's story in short writings. Part Two is everything she learned from going through a traumatic divorce while navigating new motherhood during Covid lockdown. It is a story of emotional healing and written from the heart to give back to divorcing women so they might not suffer as she did. Marianna's most heartfelt wish is to pay it forward and offer some glimmer of hope.